54 Tennis Drills for Today's Game: Improve Consistency and Power

By Joseph Correa

"This book will teach you how to become more consistent by adding spin to your shots which will give you the confidence to hit with more power."

COPYRIGHT PAGE

© 2013 54 Tennis Drills for Today's Game: Improve Consistency and Power by Joseph Correa
ISBN 978-1-941-52504-3

All rights reserved. This book or any portion thereof may not be reproduced or used in any manner without the express written permission of the publisher except for brief book quotations for reviews in the book.

Scanning, uploading, and distributing of this book via the Internet or via any other means without the express permission of the publisher and author is illegal and punishable by law.

Only purchase authorized editions of this book. Please consult with your physician before training and using this book.
You can visit the author's website at tennisvideostore.com

TABLE OF CONTENTS

Copyright Page
Introduction
About the author
Materials needed and set up

Chapter 1: Fed drills with rope
Chapter 2: Live ball drills with rope
Chapter 3: Points with rope
To Finish Off: Points without rope
More titles by Joseph Correa

CHAPTER 1: FED DRILLS

1. Hitting over the rope cross court forehand
2. Hitting over the rope cross court backhand
3. Hitting over the rope down the line forehand
4. Hitting over the rope down the line backhand
5. Hitting over the rope alternating forehand and backhand cross court
6. Hitting over the rope alternating forehand and backhand down the line
7. Hitting under the rope cross court forehands
8. Hitting under the rope cross court backhands
9. Hitting under the rope down the line forehands
10. Hitting under the rope down the line forehands
11. Hitting under the rope alternating forehands and backhands cross court
12. Hitting under the rope alternating forehands and backhands down the line

CHAPTER 2: LIVE BALL DRILLS
OVER THE ROPE

13. Over the rope 20 balls with topspin forehand to forehand cross court rally (consistency)

14. Over the rope 20 balls with topspin backhand to backhand crosscourt rally (consistency)

15. Over the rope 20 balls with topspin forehand to backhand down the line rally (consistency)

16. Over the rope 20 balls with topspin backhand to forehand down the line rally (consistency)

17. Over the rope 20 balls with one person hitting only cross court while the other does down the line shots (figure 8 consistency)

18. Over the rope 20 balls with one person hitting only down the line while the other does cross court shots (figure 8 consistency)

UNDER THE ROPE DRILLS

19. Under the rope 20 balls cross court forehand to forehand rally

20. Under the rope 20 balls cross court backhand to backhand rally

21. Under the rope 20 balls down the line forehand to backhand rally

22. Under the rope 20 balls down the line backhand to forehand rally

23. Under the rope 20 balls cross court slice backhand rally

24. Under the rope 20 balls with one person hitting cross court while the other hits only down the line to create a figure 8

25. Under the rope 20 balls with one person hitting down the line while the other hits only cross court to create a figure 8

OVER AND UNDER THE ROPE DRILLS

26. One person hits forehands over the rope with topspin while the person hits forehands under the rope cross court

27. One person hits backhands over the rope with topspin while the person hits backhands under the rope cross court

28. One person hits forehands over the rope with topspin while the person hits backhands under the rope down the line

29. One person hits backhands over the rope with topspin while the person hits forehands under the rope down the line

30. One person hits backhands over the rope with topspin while the person hits slice backhands under the rope cross court

31. One person hits forehands over the rope with topspin while the person hits forehands under the rope crosscourt inside out

CHAPTER 3: POINT DRILLS

32. Points up the 10 only over the rope without serve

33. Points up to 10 only under the rope without serve
34. Points up to 10 where one person can only hit over the rope while the other can only hit under the rope without serve
35. Points up to 10 (with serve) over the rope (serve goes under the rope at all times unless you are doing a topspin or kick serve)
36. Points up to 10 (with serve) under the rope (serve goes under the rope at all times unless you are doing a topspin or kick serve)

CHAPTER 4: NORMAL POINT DRILLS WITHOUT ROPE

37. Points up the 10 without serve only cross court forehands
38. Points up to 10 without serve only cross court backhands
39. Points up to 10 without serve only down the line backhand to forehand
40. Points up the 10 without serve only down the line forehand to backhand
41. Points up the 10 with serve only cross court forehands
42. Points up to 10 with serve only cross court backhands
43. Points up to 10 with serve only down the line backhand to forehand
44. Points up the 10 with serve only down the line forehand to backhand
45. Points up to 10 where one person can only hit cross

court and the other person can only hit down the line without serve

46. Points up to 10 where one person can only hit down the line and the other person can only hit cross court without serve

47. Points up to 10 where one person can only hit cross court and the other person can only hit down the line with serve

48. Points up to 10 where one person can only hit down the line and the other person can only hit cross court with serve

49. Points up to 10 without serve. Complete normal points without any patterns.

50. Points up to 10 with serve. Complete normal points without any patterns.

51. Play a complete set with serve playing only cross court while your partner hits only down the line.

52. Play a complete set with serve playing only down the line while your partner hits only cross court.

53. Play a complete set using any pattern you desire.

54. Play a complete match using any pattern you desire.

Would you do me a favor?

Other titles by Joseph Correa

INTRODUCTION

Point drills and advanced tennis drills are lots of fun and are exciting for the players doing them. Sometimes it might become difficult for you to complete some of the rope drills but don't give. Keep working hard and eventually you will get it right. This unusual type of training will help you to improve your overall control of high balls, low balls, high top spin, and low slice, flat or with minimal topspin. You will also improve your ability to direct the ball to specific spots on the court as well as become a lot more consistent. Once you complete this training you will feel more complete as a tennis player and will enjoy making your opponents work harder than they have ever before.

If you are beginner or intermediate in level, you can still do these drills as they can only make you better than you are right now but you might feel it requires some persistence until you get it right.

Everything here is assuming you are right handed but you can simply do the opposite if you are left handed. This was done to simplify things but applies to both right handed players and left handed players.

ABOUT THE AUTHOR

Hello, my name is Joseph Correa and I have been training and teaching tennis for over 15 years. I played professional tennis for years and am now a USPTR professional certified coach.

After years of competing and training with some of the best in the world I have learned that most people can be very successful in competition with the right mental, physical, and emotional training.

Proven scientific techniques, drills, and step by step phases must be performed to reach your peak and for that reason I have prepared the first group of training DVD's and books showing you how to reach your goals.

Through my work and teaching aids, I have helped hundreds of amateur and professional tennis player's advance with their physical, mental, and performance goals to achieve great results.

I teach you everything I know you will need to reach your goals and hope you will enjoy and share these lessons and ideas with loved ones. To learn more about the different lessons taught through my books and DVD's go to www.tennisvideostore.com. Many more books will be coming out this year with some advanced drills and techniques.

Best of luck,

Joseph

MATERIALS NEEDED AND SETUP

You will need:

1 Tennis court

1 rope long enough to be tied to both ends of the court.

Someone to feed you balls and someone to hit balls back at you for that part of the training.

Set up:
Measure about 2-3 feet from the height of the net so that you can tie the rope about this height on both sides of the fence (or other object you can use to tie around). Take a ruler and measure 2 feet above the height of the net for advanced and 3 feet for normal difficulty.

CHAPTER 1: FED DRILLS

Hitting over the rope cross court forehand

In this drill you will have to hit forehands over the rope crosscourt with top spin or flat balls that are fed to you by someone else on the other side of the net. Make sure you work on depth and control.

Hitting over the rope cross court backhand

In this drill you will have to hit backhands over the rope crosscourt with top spin or flat balls that are fed to you by someone else on the other side of the net. Make sure you work on depth and control.

Hitting over the rope down the line forehand

For this drill you should hit over the rope with top spin with your forehand down the line and have the ball land deep on the court. Make sure to focus on your follow through and to use your legs to generate spin. This can be a great offensive shot if your opponent has a weak backhand or has trouble with mid height balls or even high balls. Flat shots are allowed but this drill is most effectively done with top spin.

Hitting over the rope down the line backhand

For this drill you should hit over the rope with top spin with your backhand down the line and have the ball land deep on the court. Make sure to focus on your follow through and to use your legs to generate spin. This can be a great offensive shot if your opponent is attacking you backhand and you need to get them on the run with a safe shot. Flat shots are allowed but this drill is most effectively done with top spin.

Hitting over the rope alternating forehand and backhand cross court

For this drill you should hit over the rope with top spin with your forehand cross court and then the following shot with your backhand cross court. Continue doing this for the remainder of the drill. Work on keeping the ball deep on the court. Make sure to focus on your follow through and to use your legs to generate spin. This can be a great offensive shot if your opponent doesn't move very well. Flat shots are allowed but this drill is most effectively done with top spin.

Hitting over the rope alternating forehand and backhand down the line

For this drill you should hit over the rope with top spin with your forehand down the line and then the following shot with your backhand down the line. Continue doing this for the remainder of the drill. Work on keeping the ball deep on the court. Make sure to focus on your follow through and to use your legs to generate spin. This can be a great offensive shot if your opponent doesn't move very well. Flat shots are allowed but this drill is most effectively done with top spin. Work on keeping the ball deep on the court. Make sure to focus on your follow through and to use your legs to generate spin. This can be a great offensive shot if your opponent doesn't move very well. Flat shots are allowed but this drill is most effectively done with top spin.

Hitting under the rope cross court forehands

For this drill you should hit under the rope with top spin or flat with your forehand cross court and have the ball land deep on the court. Make sure to focus on your follow through and to use your legs to generate spin. This can be a great offensive shot if your opponent has a weaker forehand than you. Flat shots are allowed but this drill is most effectively done with top spin.

Hitting under the rope cross court backhands

For this drill you should hit under the rope with top spin or flat with your backhand cross court and have the ball land deep on the court. Make sure to focus on your follow through and to use your legs to generate spin. This can be a great offensive shot if your opponent has a weaker backhand than you. Flat shots are allowed but this drill is most effectively done with top spin.

Hitting under the rope down the line forehands

For this drill you should hit under the rope with top spin or flat with your forehand down the line and have the ball land deep on the court. Make sure to focus on your follow through and to use your legs to generate spin. This can be a great offensive shot if your opponent has a weak backhand. Flat shots are allowed but this drill is most effectively done with top spin.

Hitting under the rope down the line backhands

For this drill you should hit under the rope with top spin or flat with your backhand down the line and have the ball land deep on the court. Make sure to focus on your follow through and to use your legs to generate spin. This can be a great offensive shot if your opponent has a weak forehand on the run. Flat shots are allowed but this drill is most effectively done with top spin.

Hitting under the rope alternating forehands and backhands cross court

For this drill you should hit under the rope with top spin with your forehand cross court and then the following shot with your backhand cross court. Continue doing this for the remainder of the drill. Work on keeping the ball deep on the court. Make sure to focus on your follow through and to use your legs to generate spin. This can be a great offensive shot if your opponent doesn't move very well. Flat shots are allowed but this drill is most effectively done with top spin.

Hitting under the rope alternating forehands and backhands down the line

For this drill you should hit under the rope with top spin with your forehand down the line and then the following shot with your backhand down the line. Continue doing this for the remainder of the drill. Work on keeping the ball deep on the court. Make sure to focus on your follow through and to use your legs to generate spin. This can be a great offensive shot if your opponent doesn't move very well. Flat shots are allowed but this drill is most effectively done with top spin.

CHAPTER 2: LIVE BALL DRILLS

OVER THE ROPE
Over the rope 20 balls with topspin forehand to forehand cross court rally (consistency)

For this drill you should hit over the rope with top spin or flat with your forehand cross court and have the ball land deep on the court. Your hitting partner or coach should hit back cross court forehands to you. Your goal is to reach a minimum of 20 balls hit back and forth without missing. If you miss you have to start back at zero. Continue until you get passed 20 balls hit with this pattern. Flat shots are allowed but this drill is most effectively done with top spin.

Over the rope 20 balls with topspin backhand to backhand crosscourt rally (consistency)

For this drill you should hit over the rope with top spin or flat with your backhand cross court and have the ball land deep on the court. Your hitting partner or coach should hit back cross court backhands to you. Your goal is to reach a minimum of 20 balls hit back and forth without missing. If you miss you have to start back at zero. Continue until you get passed 20 balls hit with this pattern. Flat shots are allowed but this drill is most effectively done with top spin.

Over the rope 20 balls with topspin forehand to backhand down the line rally (consistency)

For this drill you should hit over the rope with top spin or flat with your forehand down the line and have the ball land deep on the court. Your hitting partner or coach should hit back down the line backhands to you. Your goal is to reach a minimum of 20 balls hit back and forth without missing. If you miss you have to start back at zero. Continue until you get passed 20 balls hit with this pattern. Flat shots are allowed but this drill is most effectively done with top spin.

Over the rope 20 balls with topspin backhand to forehand down the line rally (consistency)

For this drill you should hit over the rope with top spin or flat with your backhand down the line and have the ball land deep on the court. Your hitting partner or coach should hit back down the line forehands to you. Your goal is to reach a minimum of 20 balls hit back and forth without missing. If you miss you have to start back at zero. Continue until you get passed 20 balls hit with this pattern. Flat shots are allowed but this drill is most effectively done with top spin.

Over the rope 20 balls with one person hitting only cross court while the other does down the line shots (figure 8 consistency)

For this drill you should hit over the rope with top spin or flat with your forehand cross court and have the ball land deep on the court. Your hitting partner or coach should hit back down the line to your backhand. You now hit cross court to their backhand where they will return a down the line backhand to your forehand. This sequence will continue. Your goal is to reach a minimum of 20 balls hit back and forth without missing. Each ball hit counts as 1. If you miss you have to start back at zero. Continue until you get passed 20 balls hit with this pattern. Flat shots are allowed but this drill is most effectively done with top spin.

Over the rope 20 balls with one person hitting only down the line while the other does cross court shots (figure 8 consistency)

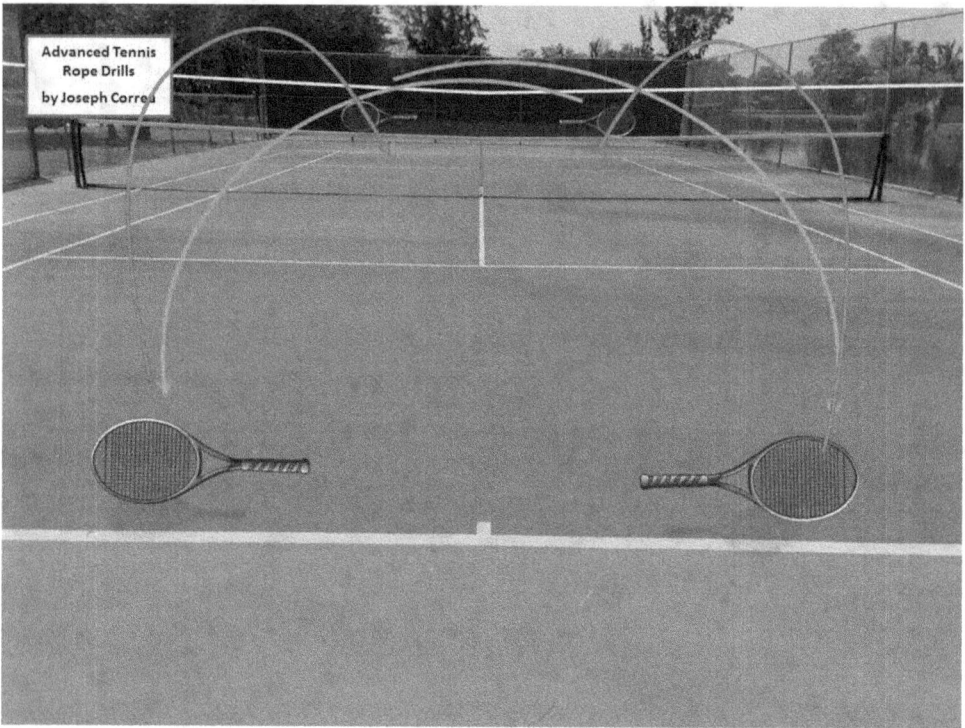

For this drill you should hit over the rope with top spin or flat with your forehand down the line and have the ball land deep on the court. Your hitting partner or coach should hit back cross court to your backhand. You now hit down the line to their backhand and they will return cross court to your forehand. This sequence will continue. Your goal is to reach a minimum of 20 balls hit back and forth without missing. Each ball hit counts as 1. If you miss you have to start back at zero. Continue until you get passed 20 balls hit with this pattern. Flat shots are allowed but this drill is most effectively done with top spin.

UNDER THE ROPE DRILLS
Under the rope 20 balls cross court forehand to forehand rally

For this drill you should hit under the rope with top spin or flat with your forehand cross court and have the ball land deep on the court. Your hitting partner or coach should hit back cross court forehands to you. Your goal is to reach a minimum of 20 balls hit back and forth without missing. If you miss you have to start back at zero. Continue until you get passed 20 balls hit with this pattern. Flat shots are allowed but this drill is most effectively done with top spin.

Under the rope 20 balls cross court backhand to backhand rally

For this drill you should hit under the rope with top spin or flat with your backhand cross court and have the ball land deep on the court. Your hitting partner or coach should hit back cross court backhands to you. Your goal is to reach a minimum of 20 balls hit back and forth without missing. If you miss you have to start back at zero. Continue until you get passed 20 balls hit with this pattern. Flat shots are allowed but this drill is most effectively done with top spin.

Under the rope 20 balls down the line forehand to backhand rally

For this drill you should hit under the rope with top spin or flat with your forehand down the line and have the ball land deep on the court. Your hitting partner or coach should hit back down the line backhands to you. Your goal is to reach a minimum of 20 balls hit back and forth without missing. If you miss you have to start back at zero. Continue until you get passed 20 balls hit with this pattern. Flat shots are allowed but this drill is most effectively done with top spin.

Under the rope 20 balls down the line backhand to forehand rally

For this drill you should hit under the rope with top spin or flat with your backhand down the line and have the ball land deep on the court. Your hitting partner or coach should hit back down the line forehands to you. Your goal is to reach a minimum of 20 balls hit back and forth without missing. If you miss you have to start back at zero. Continue until you get passed 20 balls hit with this pattern. Flat shots are allowed but this drill is most effectively done with top spin.

Under the rope 20 balls cross court slice backhand rally

For this drill you should hit under the rope with slice with your backhand cross court and your hitting partner or coach should hit back slice cross court. Your goal is to reach a minimum of 20 balls hit back and forth without missing. If you miss you have to start back at zero. Continue until you get passed 20 balls hit with this pattern.

Under the rope 20 balls with one person hitting cross court while the other hits only down the line to create a figure 8

For this drill you should hit under the rope with top spin or flat with your forehand cross court. Your hitting partner or coach should hit back down the line to your backhand. You now hit cross court to their backhand where they will return a down the line backhand to your forehand. This sequence will continue. Your goal is to reach a minimum of 20 balls hit back and forth without missing. Each ball hit counts as 1. If you miss you have to start back at zero. Continue until you get passed 20 balls hit with this pattern. Flat shots are allowed but this drill is most effectively done with top spin.

Under the rope 20 balls with one person hitting down the line while the other hits only cross court to create a figure 8

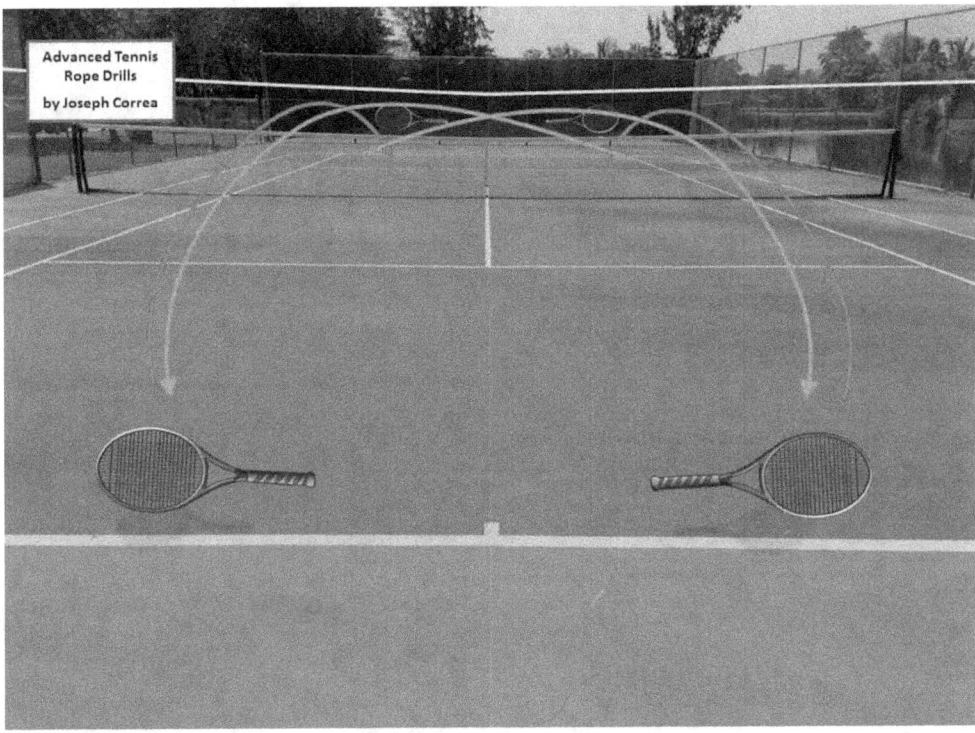

For this drill you should hit under the rope with top spin or flat with your forehand down the line and have the ball land deep on the court. Your hitting partner or coach should hit back cross court to your backhand. You now hit down the line to their backhand and they will return cross court to your forehand. This sequence will continue. Your goal is to reach a minimum of 20 balls hit back and forth without missing. Each ball hit counts as 1. If you miss you have to start back at zero. Continue until you get passed 20 balls hit with this pattern. Flat shots are allowed but this drill is most effectively done with top spin.

54 Tennis Drills for Today's Game: Improve Consistency and Power

OVER AND UNDER THE ROPE DRILLS

One person hits forehands over the rope with topspin while the person hits forehands under the rope cross court

For this drill you should ht over the rope with top spin or flat with your forehand cross court and have the ball land deep on the court. Your hitting partner or coach should hit back cross court forehands under the rope back to you. Your goal is to reach a minimum of 20 balls hit back and forth without missing. If you miss you have to start back at zero. Continue until you get passed 20 balls hit with this pattern. Flat shots are allowed but this drill is most effectively done with top spin.

One person hits backhands over the rope with topspin while the person hits backhands under the rope cross court

For this drill you should hit over the rope with top spin or flat with your backhand cross court and have the ball land deep on the court. Your hitting partner or coach should hit back cross court backhands under the rope back to you. Your goal is to reach a minimum of 20 balls hit back and forth without missing. If you miss you have to start back at zero. Continue until you get passed 20 balls hit with this pattern. Flat shots are allowed but this drill is most effectively done with top spin.

One person hits forehands over the rope with topspin while the person hits backhands under the rope down the line

For this drill you should hit over the rope with top spin or flat with your forehand down the line and have the ball land deep on the court. Your hitting partner or coach should hit back down the line backhands under the rope back to you. Your goal is to reach a minimum of 20 balls hit back and forth without missing. If you miss you have to start back at zero. Continue until you get passed 20 balls hit with this pattern. Flat shots are allowed but this drill is most effectively done with top spin.

One person hits backhands over the rope with topspin while the person hits forehands under the rope down the line

For this drill you should hit over the rope with top spin or flat with your backhand down the line and have the ball land deep on the court. Your hitting partner or coach should hit back down the line forehands under the rope back to you. Your goal is to reach a minimum of 20 balls hit back and forth without missing. If you miss you have to start back at zero. Continue until you get passed 20 balls hit with this pattern. Flat shots are allowed but this drill is most effectively done with top spin.

54 Tennis Drills for Today's Game: Improve Consistency and Power

One person hits backhands over the rope with topspin while the person hits slice backhands under the rope cross court

For this drill you should hit over the rope with top spin or flat with your backhand cross court and have the ball land deep on the court. Your hitting partner or coach should hit back cross court slices under the rope back to you. Your goal is to reach a minimum of 20 balls hit back and forth without missing. If you miss you have to start back at zero. Continue until you get passed 20 balls hit with this pattern. Flat shots are allowed but this drill is most effectively done with top spin.

One person hits forehands over the rope with topspin while the person hits forehands under the rope crosscourt inside out

For this drill you should hit over the rope with top spin or flat with your forehand down the line from the backhand corner and have the ball land deep on the court. Your hitting partner or coach should hit back down the line forehands under the rope back to you. Your goal is to reach a minimum of 20 balls hit back and forth without missing. If you miss you have to start back at zero. Continue until you get passed 20 balls hit with this pattern. Flat shots are allowed but this drill is most effectively done with top spin.

CHAPTER 3: POINT DRILLS

Points up to 10 only over the rope without serve

Play up to 10 points with the winner reaching 10 while hitting only over the rope.

Points up to 10 only under the rope without serve

Play up to 10 points with the winner reaching 10 while hitting only under the rope.

Points up to 10 where one person can only hit over the rope while the other can only hit under the rope without serve

Play up to 10 points with the winner reaching 10 while hitting only over the rope for one person and under the rope for the other person.

Points up to 10 (with serve) over the rope (serve goes under the rope at all times unless you are doing topspin or kick serve)

Play up to 10 points with the winner reaching 10 while hitting only over the rope and starting the point with a serve that should always go under the rope.

Points up to 10 (with serve) under the rope (serve goes under the rope at all times unless you are doing topspin or kick serve)

Play up to 10 points with the winner reaching 10 while hitting only under the rope and starting the point with a serve that should always go under the rope.

CHAPTER 4: NORMAL POINT DRILLS WITHOUT ROPE

37. Points up the 10 without serve only cross court forehands

Feed the ball under hand to your opponent's forehand and then play the point cross court only as to have both of you hitting only cross court until one of you wins the point with a winner or one of you misses and hits to the net or out. Remember that if one or both of you are left handed please make the necessary adjustments to this drill. The first person to reach 10 points wins. There is no "difference of two points" structure in these drills.

38. Points up to 10 without serve only cross court backhands

Feed the ball under hand to your opponent's backhand and then play the point cross court only as to have both of you hitting only cross court until one of you wins the point with a winner or one of you misses and hits to the net or out. Remember that if one or both of you are left handed please make the necessary adjustments to this drill. The first person to reach 10 points wins. There is no "difference of two points" structure in these drills.

39. Points up to 10 without serve only down the line backhand to forehand

Feed the ball under hand to your opponent's forehand and then play the point down the line only as to have both of you hitting until one of you wins the point with a winner or one of you misses and hits to the net or out. Remember that if one or both of you are left handed please make the necessary adjustments to this drill. The first person to reach 10 points wins. There is no "difference of two points" structure in these drills.

40. Points up the 10 without serve only down the line forehand to backhand

Feed the ball under hand to your opponent's backhand and then play the point down the line only as to have both of you hitting until one of you wins the point with a winner or one of you misses and hits to the net or out. Remember that if one or both of you are left handed please make the necessary adjustments to this drill. The first person to reach 10 points wins. There is no "difference of two points" structure in these drills.

41. Points up the 10 with serve only cross court forehands

Serve the ball to your opponent's forehand and then play the point cross court only as to have both of you hitting only cross court until one of you wins the point with a winner or one of you misses and hits to the net or out. Remember that if one or both of you are left handed please make the necessary adjustments to this drill. The first person to reach 10 points wins. There is no "difference of two points" structure in these drills.

42. Points up to 10 with serve only cross court backhands

Serve the ball to your opponent's backhand and then play the point cross court only as to have both of you hitting only cross court until one of you wins the point with a winner or one of you misses and hits to the net or out. Remember that if one or both of you are left handed please make the necessary adjustments to this drill. The first person to reach 10 points wins. There is no "difference of two points" structure in these drills.

43. Points up to 10 with serve only down the line backhand to forehand

Serve the ball to your opponent's forehand and then play the point down the line only as to have both of you hitting until one of you wins the point with a winner or one of you misses and hits to the net or out. Remember that if one or both of you are left handed please make the necessary adjustments to this drill. The first person to reach 10 points wins. There is no "difference of two points" structure in these drills.

44. Points up the 10 with serve only down the line forehand to backhand

Serve the ball to your opponent's backhand and then play the point down the line only as to have both of you hitting until one of you wins the point with a winner or one of you misses and hits to the net or out. Remember that if one or both of you are left handed please make the necessary adjustments to this drill. The first person to reach 10 points wins. There is no "difference of two points" structure in these drills.

45. Points up to 10 where one person can only hit cross court and the other person can only hit down the line without serve

Feed the ball under hand to your opponent's forehand and then play the point cross court only as to have both of you hitting only cross court until one of you wins the point with a winner or one of you misses and hits to the net or out. Remember that if one or both of you are left handed please make the necessary adjustments to this drill. The first person to reach 10 points wins. There is no "difference of two points" structure in these drills.

46. Points up to 10 where one person can only hit down the line and the other person can only hit cross court without serve

Feed the ball under hand to your opponent's forehand and then play the point cross court only as to have both of you hitting only cross court until one of you wins the point with a winner or one of you misses and hits to the net or out. Remember that if one or both of you are left handed please make the necessary adjustments to this drill. The first person to reach 10 points wins. There is no "difference of two points" structure in these drills.

47. Points up to 10 where one person can only hit cross court and the other person can only hit down the line with serve

Serve the ball to your opponent and then play the point cross court while your partner hits only down the line as to create a figure 8. Keep the ball in play until one of you wins the point with a winner or one of you misses and hits to the net or out. Remember that if one or both of you are left handed please make the necessary adjustments to this drill. The first person to reach 10 points wins. There is no "difference of two points" structure in these drills.

48. Points up to 10 where one person can only hit down the line and the other person can only hit cross court with serve

Serve the ball to your opponent and then play the point cross court while your partner hits only down the line as to create a figure 8. Keep the ball in play until one of you wins the point with a winner or one of you misses and hits to the net or out. Remember that if one or both of you are left handed please make the necessary adjustments to this drill. The first person to reach 10 points wins. There is no "difference of two points" structure in these drills.

49. Points up to 10 without serve. Complete normal points without any patterns.
Feed the ball to your opponent under hand and then play the point normally without any required patterns. Keep the ball in play until one of you wins the point with a winner or one of you misses and hits to the net or out. Remember that if one or both of you are left handed please make the necessary adjustments to this drill. The first person to reach 10 points wins. There is no "difference of two points" structure in these drills.

50. Points up to 10 with serve. Complete normal points without any patterns.
Serve the ball to your opponent and then play the point without any required patterns. Keep the ball in play until one of you wins the point with a winner or one of you misses and hits to the net or out. Remember that if one or both of you are left handed please make the necessary adjustments to this drill. The first person to reach 10 points wins. There is no "difference of two points" structure in these drills.

51. Play a complete set with serve playing only cross court while your partner hits only down the line.
52. Play a complete set with serve playing only down the line while your partner hits only cross court.
53. Play a complete set using any pattern you desire.
54. Play a complete match using any pattern you desire.

WOULD YOU DO ME A FAVOR?

Thank you for downloading and reading this book. I hope it was helpful and at least one thing makes you win an extra match or two.

I have a small favor to ask. Would you mind writing a short comment and rate this book on www.amazon.com?

I like to read all the reviews on my books and enjoy knowing what others think of this book. I feel the best pay comes from good positive reviews from tennis enthusiasts that enjoyed reading it.

You can complete your review on Amazon.com under Advanced Tennis Rope Drills by Joseph Correa.

If you know of a family member or friend, that you think would benefit from reading this book, please take a minute to share it with them so that they may improve their game as well. I enjoy helping others and would like to answer questions free of charge. You can Tweet me on www.twitter.com at @mybetterswing.com
Check out some of my other books on the next page.

OTHER TITLES BY JOSEPH CORREA

Tennis Serve Harder Training Program
This DVD will teach you how to serve 10-20 mph faster in a 3 month day by day program. The best serve training program in the market. Video includes a 3 month chart training program and a step by step manual. The DVD shows you how to do the exercises properly and the process you should follow in order to be successful with the program.

Joseph Correa is a professional tennis player and coach that has competed and taught all over the world in ITF and ATP tournaments for many years. Besides being a professional tennis player he has a USPTR professional coaching certification and ITF kids coaching certification.

The 33 Laws of Tennis
The 33 Laws of Tennis is book full of valuable tennis concepts to help you become a better and more prepared tennis player. Written by a professional tennis player and coach in the USA. It's a very useful book that will come in handy when you least expect it and will remind you of many little but important things before competing.
Tennis Footwork and Cardio by Joseph Correa
Joseph Correa is a professional tennis player and coach that has competed and taught all over the world in ITF and ATP tournaments for many years. Besides being a professional tennis player he has a USPTR professional coaching certification and ITF kids coaching certification.

Get in better shape and improve your mobility on and off the tennis court. Your foot work will improve drastically as well as strengthen your core and upper body. This is definitely worthwhile for a serious tennis player no matter what your level. You become faster, stronger, and more agile and on the court as well as seeing an increase in acceleration in your groundstrokes and serve. Created by a professional tennis player for others to advance in their game and win more matches.

Yoga Tennis by Joseph Correa
Yoga Tennis by Joseph Correa is a great way to improve your flexibility and agility on the court. Reach more balls and have fewer injuries. It's a great way to win more by working on a different part of your game. The DVD lasts about 30 minutes. Used by amateur and professional tennis players to improve their game and last longer in matches. This is the best way for a tennis player to become more flexible and get rid of common back, knee, shoulder, hamstring, calf, and quadriceps injuries. You´ll be glad to get started! This is an improved version of our MBS Yoga Tennis 2012.

The Vilcabamba Diet
The best diet and exercise book you will find if you want to get in shape and live longer. It's based on a village in Ecuador called "Vilcabamba" where most of its inhabitants live longer than the average person and in great condition. Great for athletes!

Tennis Abs by Joseph Correa
Tennis Abs is a great way to strengthen your core for

more powerful serves, forehands and backhands as well as stronger volleys. Abdominals are fundamental for a better game. This DVD works on many types of crunches, sit-ups, and lateral abs and back exercises that you won't find in other abdominal videos. Feel confident when changing your shirt during your match and hit the ball harder!

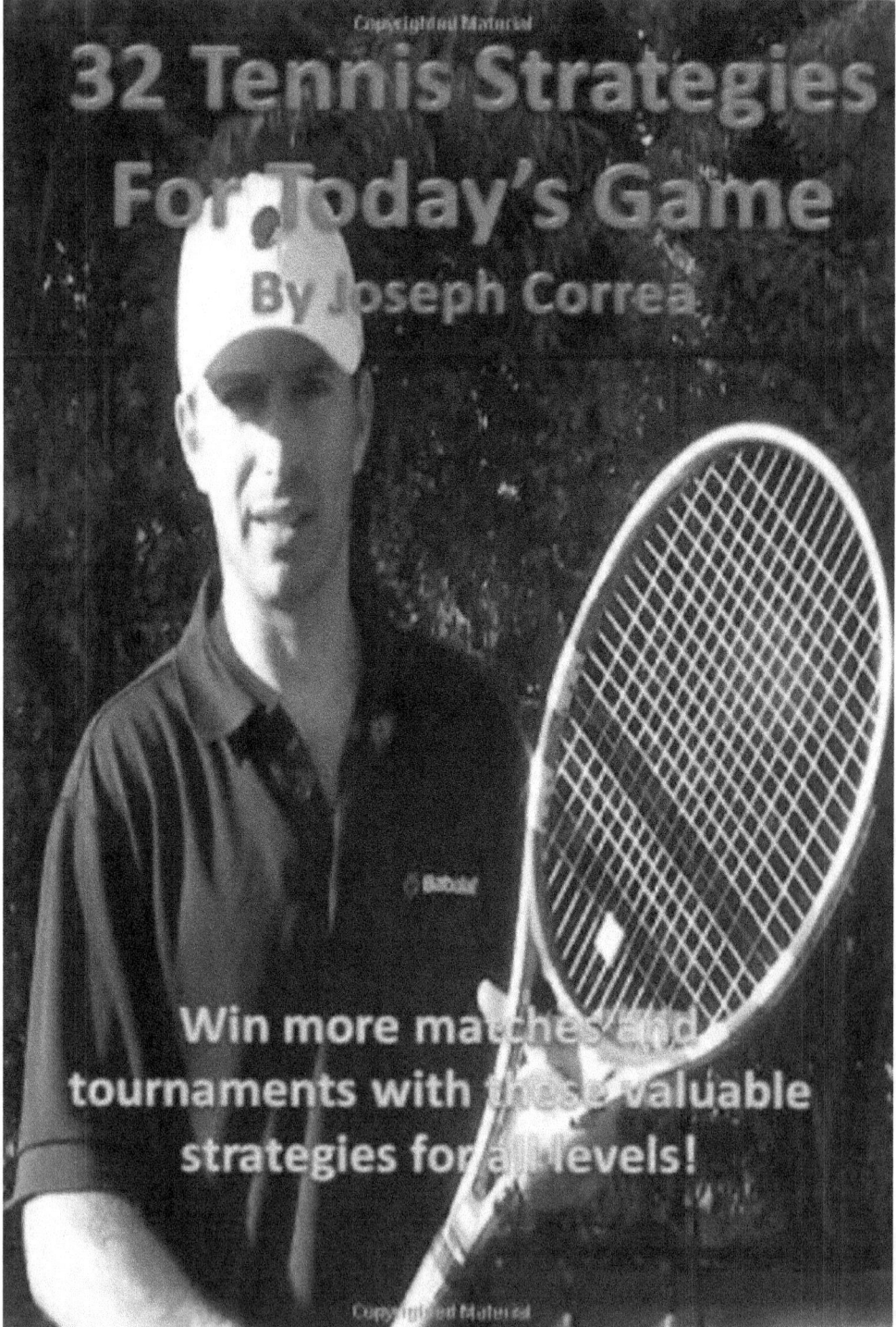

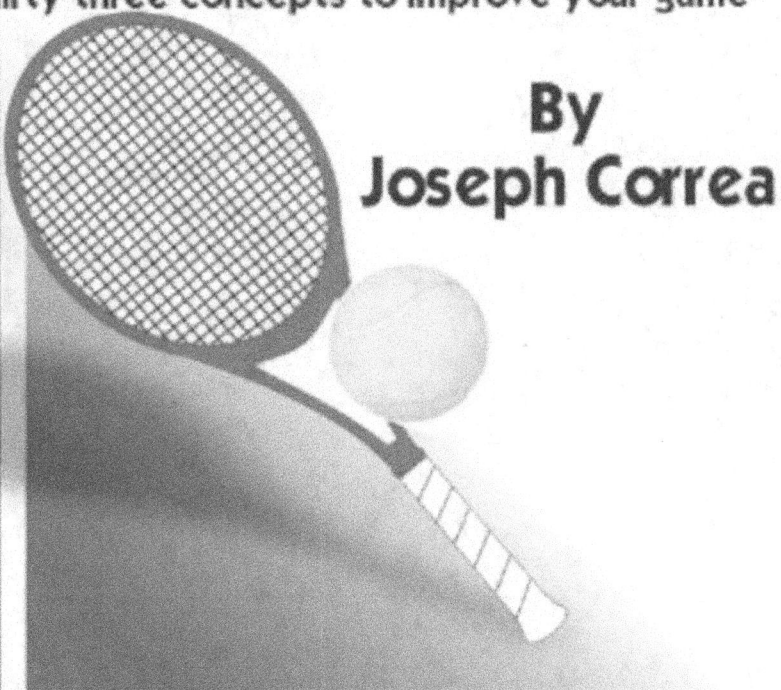

TENNIS FOOTWORK AND CARDIO

BY JOSEPH CORREA©

This video will improve your flexibility, agility and balance on and off the court with some awsome results. Used by professional tennis players and amateurs.

1 DVD

THE VILCABAMBA DIET

Learn how to live longer and healthier like the people of Vilcabamba!

This book includes: 101 Exercises You Can Do Any Time & Any Place plus BONUS ABS

By
Joseph G. Correa

In Collaboration With
Dr. Juan Carlos Correa

AB TRAINING
By Joseph Correa ©

Ab training for athletes of all levels!

12 Tennis Secrets to Win More

by Joseph Correa

"What you should be doing and working on to win all the time!"

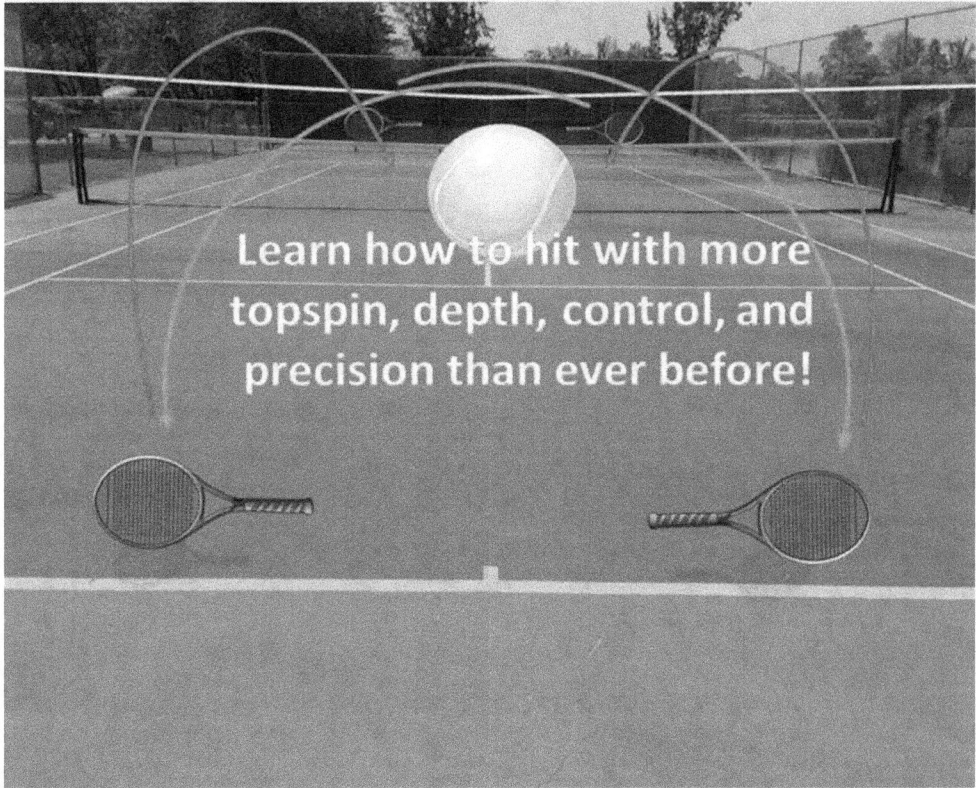

Superman Tennis Serve

Learn how to serve your fastest serve ever through scientifically proven techniques!

By Joseph Correa

DR. JUAN CARLOS CORREA and JOSEPH CORREA

The Vilcabamba Diet :

Lose 10 pounds or more!

Lose Weight, Live Longer, and Eat Healthier with the Magic Formula of our Ancestors

www.ingramcontent.com/pod-product-compliance
Lightning Source LLC
Chambersburg PA
CBHW071221070526
44584CB00019B/3108